D1607224

# TODD GURLEY

## SUPERSTAR RUNNING BACK

BIG BUDDY

★ NFL ★
SUPERSTARS

DENNIS ST. SAUVER

**abdobooks.com**

Published by Abdo Publishing, a division of ABDO, PO Box 398166, Minneapolis, Minnesota 55439.
Copyright © 2020 by Abdo Consulting Group, Inc. International copyrights reserved in all countries.
No part of this book may be reproduced in any form without written permission from the publisher.
Big Buddy Books™ is a trademark and logo of Abdo Publishing.

Printed in the United States of America, North Mankato, Minnesota.
052019
092019

Cover Photo: Dilip Vishwanat/Getty Images; efks/Getty Images.
Interior Photos: Al Bello/Getty Images (p. 29); Alan Campbell/AP Images (p. 9); Casey Rodgers/AP
    Images (p. 25); Ezra Shaw/Getty Images (p. 5); Jonathan Daniel/Getty Images (p. 13); Omar
    Vega/AP Images (p. 17); Otto Greule Jr/Getty Images (p. 27); Rich Graessle/AP Images (p. 23);
    Scott Cunningham/Getty Images (p. 11); Steve Dykes/Getty Images (pp. 15, 19); Wesley Hitt/
    Getty Images (p. 21).

Coordinating Series Editor: Elizabeth Andrews
Graphic Design: Jenny Christensen, Cody Laberda

Library of Congress Control Number: 2018967165

Publisher's Cataloging-in-Publication Data

Names: St. Sauver, Dennis, author.
Title: Todd Gurley: superstar running back / by Dennis St. Sauver
Other title: Superstar running back
Description: Minneapolis, Minnesota : Abdo Publishing, 2020 | Series: NFL superstars |
    Includes online resources and index.
Identifiers: ISBN 9781532119828 (lib. bdg.) | ISBN 9781532174582 (ebook)
Subjects: LCSH: Running backs (Football)--Juvenile literature. | Football players--United
    States--Biography--Juvenile literature. | Los Angeles Rams (Football team : 2016-)--
    Juvenile literature. | Sports--Biography--Juvenile literature.
Classification: DDC 796.3326409 [B]--dc23

# CONTENTS

★ ★ ★     ★ ★ ★

Superstar Running Back ............... 4

Snapshot ................................. 5

Early Years .............................. 6

Starting Out ............................. 8

Big Dreams ............................. 12

Going Pro .............................. 14

A Rising Star .......................... 18

Off The Field .......................... 22

Giving Back ........................... 24

Awards ................................. 26

Buzz .................................... 28

Glossary ............................... 30

Online Resources ..................... 31

Index ................................... 32

# SUPERSTAR RUNNING BACK

Todd Gurley is a star running back in the National Football League (NFL). He plays for the Los Angeles Rams in California.

Since 2015, Todd has left his mark as one of the best football players in the league. After a strong 2018 season, he helped lead his team to the Super Bowl.

# SNAPSHOT

**NAME:**
Todd Gerome
Gurley II

**BIRTHDAY:**
August 3, 1994

**BIRTHPLACE:**
Baltimore, Maryland

**POSITION:**
Running Back

**COLLEGE TEAM:**
University of Georgia Bulldogs

**CURRENT TEAM:**
Los Angeles Rams

# EARLY YEARS

Todd was named after his father, Todd Gerome. His mother's name is Darlene Simmons. He has four brothers named Davon, Princeton, Shannon, and Tarik. He also has one sister named Devin.

Todd played on his brother's football team when he was young. Most of the boys were two years older than Todd. Even so, he quickly became the star.

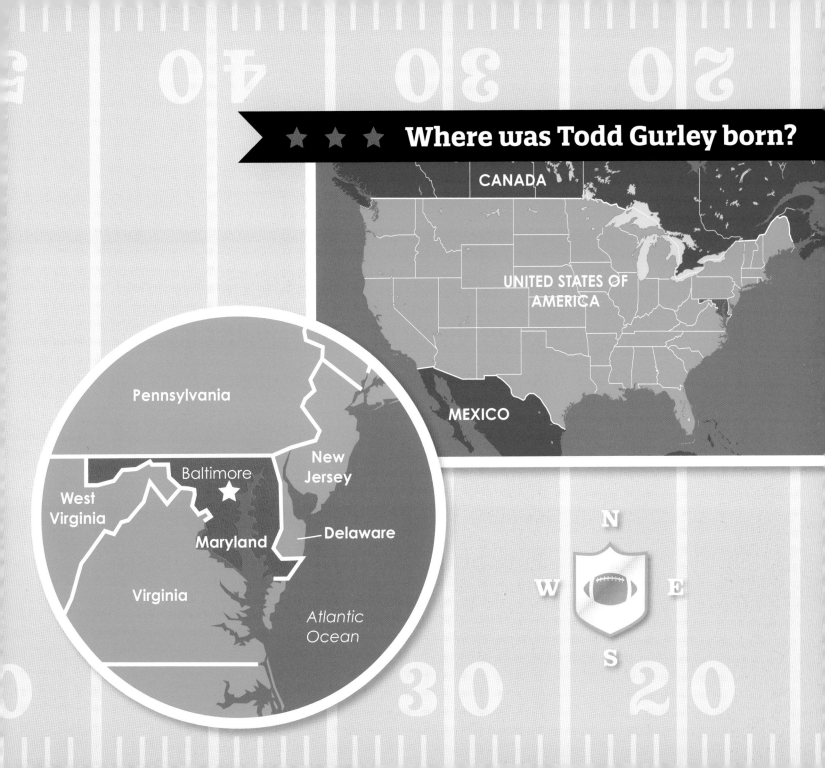

**Where was Todd Gurley born?**

CANADA

UNITED STATES OF AMERICA

MEXICO

Pennsylvania

West Virginia

Baltimore

New Jersey

Maryland

Delaware

Virginia

Atlantic Ocean

N
W E
S

# STARTING OUT

Todd attended Tarboro High School in North Carolina. He was very good at basketball, football, and track. In track, Todd was a hurdler and sprinter. He once ran the 100-meter dash in 10.7 seconds. That is very fast!

But Todd's best sport was football. By the end of high school, Todd had **rushed** for more than 4,000 yards (3,658 m) and 64 touchdowns.

In high school, Todd was rated the fifth-best running back in the country among other high school seniors.

Todd continued to improve. He attended the University of Georgia in 2012.

He was the second freshman at the university to **rush** for more than 1,000 yards (914 m). That was the best performance at Georgia since 1980. For his efforts, he was named to the Freshman **All-American** team at the end of his first season.

**DID YOU KNOW?**

Todd played both running back and safety for his high school football team. As safety, he had 79 tackles in his junior year.

Todd was a four-star recruit as he finished high school. That means many different college teams wanted him to play for them.

# BIG DREAMS

Throughout his college **career**, Todd recorded more than 3,000 **rushing** yards (2,743 m). And he scored 36 rushing touchdowns for his team.

In 2012 and 2013, Todd earned a spot on the All-Southeastern **Conference** first team. After his junior year, he decided to leave college and join the 2015 NFL **Draft**. He wanted to play **professional** football.

Todd was the first running back to be chosen in the 2015 NFL Draft.

# GOING PRO

The St. Louis Rams selected Todd tenth in the **draft**. In his **rookie** year, he scored ten touchdowns.

That same season, Todd **rushed** for 566 yards (518 m) in his first four games as a starter. That set an NFL record!

**DID YOU KNOW?**

Todd's first professional team was the St. Louis Rams. The Rams moved to Los Angeles, California, in 2016.

Todd was named the AP Offensive Rookie of the Year in 2015.

Todd continued to star for the Rams. In 2017, he **rushed** for more than 1,300 yards (1,189 m) and led the NFL in rushing touchdowns. That same year, Todd was named the NFL Offensive Player of the Year.

In January 2018, Todd played in his first **playoff** game. He carried the ball 14 times for 101 yards (92 m). The Rams lost to the Atlanta Falcons, but Todd played a very good game.

In 2017, Todd was named FedEx Ground Player of the Year.

# A RISING STAR

Sean McVay is the Rams coach. He was hired in 2017. He and Todd made a perfect match for the Rams. Sean **focused** on the offense to improve the team. Todd became one of the leaders in that plan.

In the 2018 regular season, the Rams won 13 games and lost only three. Todd helped his team win throughout the season.

Both Sean *(right)* and Todd had a great year in 2017. Sean was named NFL Coach of the Year. Todd earned Offensive Player of the Year.

Todd continues to excite his coaches, fans, and teammates. He is a fast runner and he has **rushed** for more than 4,500 yards (4,115 m) throughout his **career**.

He is also a good, strong blocker when needed. Todd has good hands to catch the ball when the quarterback throws tricky **passes**.

**DID YOU KNOW?**

Todd's teammates say that he is funny and easy to get along with.

In a 2017 game against the Tennessee Titans, Todd ran 21 miles (33.8 km) per hour for a touchdown reception!

# OFF THE FIELD

In Todd's free time, he enjoys being with his family and friends. When he spends time with his family, he does not always have to think about football.

Todd is a huge basketball fan. He likes to sit back and watch teams play. He catches the Duke Blue Devils' games whenever he gets the chance.

More than $50,000 has been given to Shriners Hospital for Children in Todd Gurley's name.

# GIVING BACK

Todd took part in the NFL's My Cause, My **Cleats** program. On December 16, 2018, he wore cleats with details from the book *The Magician's Hat* during the game.

The running back works with reading programs to raise **awareness** about childhood learning. He believes all children should have equal **access** to education.

Todd teamed up with Pizza Hut and BOOK IT! to help in his community. His goal is to inspire kids to read more.

# AWARDS

In his first year in the NFL, Todd earned the Offensive **Rookie** of the Year Award. That year, he was also named to the **Pro Bowl**.

In 2017 and 2018, he led the league in **rushing** touchdowns. For his efforts, he was Player of the Month three times during those years. He was also selected to the Pro Bowl in those seasons.

Todd scored a touchdown in 11 straight games in 2018. That tied a Rams record.

# BUZZ

Todd helped lead his team to the Super Bowl against the New England Patriots. The game was played in February 2019 in Atlanta, Georgia. Sadly, the Rams lost the game, 13-3.

The running back has helped the Rams win many games since 2015. Fans expect he will continue his success for years to come.

Todd was hurt in December 2018. He was able to get back on the field to help the Rams win the NFC title game against the Saints in January.

# GLOSSARY

**access** the right or ability to approach, enter, or use.

**All-American** selected as one of the best in the US in a particular sport.

**awareness** knowledge and understanding that something is happening or exists.

**career** a period of time spent in a certain job.

**cleats** a strip fastened to the bottom of a shoe to prevent slipping.

**conference** a group of sports teams that play against each other and that are part of a larger league of teams.

**draft** a system for professional sports teams to choose new players.

**focus** (FOH-kuhs) to give attention to.

**pass** to throw the football in the direction of the opponent's goal.

**playoff** a game or series of games to determine a championship or break a tie.

**Pro Bowl** a game that features the best players in the NFL. It does not count toward regular-season records.

**professional** (pruh-FEHSH-nuhl) paid to do a sport or activity.

**rookie** a player who is new to the NFL until he meets certain criteria.

**rush** to advance a football by running plays.

## ONLINE RESOURCES

**Booklinks**
NONFICTION NETWORK
FREE! ONLINE NONFICTION RESOURCES

To learn more about Todd Gurley, please visit **abdobooklinks.com** or scan this QR code. These links are routinely monitored and updated to provide the most current information available.

# ★ ★ ★ INDEX ★ ★ ★

awards **10, 15, 16, 17, 19, 26**

basketball **8, 22**

California **4, 14**

charity **23, 24, 25**

draft **12, 13, 14**

family **6, 22**

fans **20, 28**

Georgia **28**

league **4, 26, 29**

*Magician's Hat, The* (book) **24**

Maryland **5**

McVay, Sean **18, 19**

North Carolina **8**

Pizza Hut **25**

playoffs **16**

Pro Bowl **26**

records **9, 10, 14, 27**

Super Bowl **4, 28, 29**

teams **4, 5, 10, 11, 14, 16, 21, 22, 28, 29**

track **8**

University of Georgia **5, 10, 12**